How Can I Please You, God ?

Story by
Beverly Capps Burgess

Illustrations by
Vici McKee

All Scripture quotations are taken from
the *Amplified Version* of the Bible.

How Can I Please You, God?
ISBN 0-9618975-1-1
Copyright © 1989 By Beverly Capps Burgess
P.O. Box 520
Broken Arrow, OK 74013

Published by Annette Capps Ministries, Inc.
P.O. Box 10
Broken Arrow, OK 74013

How Can I Please You, God ?

More than anything else in the world,
There is one thing I want to do –

I want to ask You a question, God: "How can I please You?"

Maybe if I were taller,
Or just grown up a little more –

And had a family of my own,
Then I could please You more.

If I could just run to Jesus,
The first thing I would do –

Is ask Him the same question:
"How can I please You?"

Is it pleasing the way I talk and think?
Do You like the pajamas I wear –

Does it make You smile a little,
When You hear me say my prayers?

When I obey my mom,
And go to sleep when she asks me to –

Does it really make You happy?
God, how can I please You?

When I go to church on Sunday morning,
And hear the Word of God that's true –

Then I learn to read my Bible each day,
And I want to become more like You!

THAT'S what makes You HAPPY, Lord,
When I act just like You do –

I can be myself and love everyone else.
GOD, THAT'S HOW I WILL PLEASE YOU!

Therefore be imitators of God — copy Him *and* follow His example — as well-beloved children [imitate their father].

And walk in love — esteeming and delighting in one another — as Christ loved us and gave Himself up for us...

— Ephesians 5:1-2a *Amplified*